Drama verses Sketches

VERSES AND SKETCHES TO USE IN YOUTH, SEEKER, ALTERNATIVE AND ALL-AGE WORSHIP

by Steve Tilley and Bob Clucas

with additional material by
Simon Marshall and Dave Gatward

CONTENTS

INTRODUCTION TO SKETCHES

Good dramas ask questions rather than answer them. Some of the dramas in this book do that. Others merely seek to entertain or introduce a theme.

The meaning of one or two of the sketches is unclear. To some extent we go along with Andy Warhol who said, 'If I knew what it meant I wouldn't have painted it,' or something like that and it may not have been him. If we knew what some of these sketches meant we wouldn't have written them as sketches. If you want us to speak to you clearly then invite us to preach – we all do it.

There are a couple of sketches where we're grinding an axe. We're not sure if we're sharpening it or blunting it but there's definitely a rasping noise.

The sketches are quite straightforward to perform. Most require only two actors and few props. Whilst excellent drama involves being liberated from the script (so learn it) some of these could be done holding it and reading. Some are designed to look as if the players should be holding a clipboard. Clever, eh?

Casting is very important for success (just ask an angler or someone in orthopaedics). Much humour can be obtained by casting well-known church characters in incongruous roles. The minister's wife/husband as Pontius Pilate will get a laugh in most churches. If you worship at the type of church where laughter is banned you may regret the purchase of this book. Never mind. Regret is just one of the many back doors to change.

There is, though, no substitute for talent. Try to use people in sketches who have the mysterious 'it'. The sort of people you look at and say, 'I don't know what "it" is but they've certainly got it.' 'It' can't be learned but it can be developed. Be willing to be surprised by talent developing where you don't expect it, especially in teenagers. If you don't give them a chance to try, it won't. Whatever 'it' is, it includes good ....
.... timing. That joke works better verbally.

Stage directions have been kept to a minimum. That doesn't mean the sketches should be performed without any action. It means you have to work it out for yourself. Most of the characters in the sketches can be male or female. You may want to adapt the material in other ways to fit your local situation. Feel free.

If you use drama regularly, it is worth collecting together a props box. We've suggested some sound effects (**FX**). Recorded effects are available from record shops and libraries.

In many of the sketches you will find a fairly obvious Bible reading as a companion. Decide if you want to place the sketch before or after the reading. Drama is not meant to be a substitute for Bible reading.

NOAH GOES SHOPPING

CAST
Noah and a DIY super-store assistant

SCENE
A DIY Superstore

PRODUCTION NOTES
Props
• anything to suggest a DIY store
FX
• sound of thunder

BIBLE REFERENCE
Genesis 6

Assistant Do you need any help here?

Noah Thank you, yes. I'm looking for some wood.

Assistant Well you are in the timber section. Care to narrow it down a bit?

Noah Cypress wood.

Assistant Not a lot of people gopher cypress wood these days. It's not popular.

Noah No not poplar; I want cypress wood. *Cupressus semper-virens* not *Populus euphratica*.

Assistant We don't stock it. It would need to be a special order. It's not usually worth our while. How much do you need?

Noah (*Tentatively*) 56,000 … cubits?

Assistant (*Intake of breath, pause*) Well I'm sure we'd like to help sir. What's it for?

Noah I'm building an ark.

Assistant A nark. What's a nark?

Noah It's a sort of a boat.

Assistant That's a big boat.

Noah Er, yes. It's a special commission.

Assistant Oh! So you're a boat builder.

Noah Er, no. But the, er, customer gave full instructions.

Assistant Instructions? What is this? Some sort of self-assembly boat?

Noah Well it's not exactly flat-pack, but I do have a plan, and it has to be cypress wood and pitch. (*Sound of thunder offstage*) I'd like to get a move on. Can I put an order in?

Assistant Sure. It will take a week or so.

Noah Fine, er, do you do interest-free?

Assistant Of course. In fact you can have it on 'Buy now; pay next year' if you want.

Noah Er, yes please.

CHILDLINE

Counsellor Good morning, Childline. How may I help you?

No it's OK. You needn't be nervous. What did you want to talk about?

Yes.

Yes.

I see.

And what exactly did your Daddy do to you?

He took you for a trip into the mountains. That sounds really nice. What happened there?

I see. He decided to make a fire.

Right. And then?

(With emphasis) No? He made you carry all the wood. What was he carrying?

A large knife and a flaming torch? I see. So what happened?

He built an altar? How do you do that?

You get a bit of stone and lie it flat on two other stones then you put the wood on top. I see. You seem to know a lot about that sort of thing.

I see. Your Dad must be a bit fanatical about his religion.

Right. There's been 'a whole lot of other weird stuff too'. So where did we get to? You've carried a load of wood up a mountain and your Dad's built this altar thing. OK. Then what?

He never? He tied you up?

… and he put you on the altar?

… and he lifted the knife up in the air?

… and… and…?

And then he changed his mind. Are you sure you weren't hurt?

'The only scars are psychological.' Right. Are you by any chance from a religious group where child sacrifice is common?

Well, a lot of gods *do* seem to like it. We hear of many children who suffer as you have done – though, come to think of it, you're the first who's ever phoned in afterwards. Did your Dad say anything about what he'd done?

He said to help him get a ram out of a bush because it was stuck.

He made you watch while he slaughtered the ram and burnt it. That's terrible.

Oh that's perfectly normal behaviour for your family is it? I see. Do you want me to take any action?

Right. So if anybody else phones I can tell them that *your* God does not require child sacrifices. OK. That might make your God quite popular round here.

CAST
Childline telephone counsellor

SCENE
Telephone switchboard desk

PRODUCTION NOTES
The counsellor should pause between lines, as if the other person was speaking.

Props
• a phone or hands-free device with headset

BIBLE REFERENCE
Genesis 22:1-19

NOISE

CAST
Councillor Abey,
Councillor Seedee and
other councillors
(optional)

SCENE
A meeting of the
Jericho Noise
Abatement Society

PRODUCTION NOTES
Ideally, the two speaking councillors should have strong regional accents (Yorkshire, Geordie, Brummie or Scouse would all be good). Other non-speaking councillors can simply murmur, grunt and nod from time to time.

FX
• theme music from
The Great Escape on
tape or whistled/
hummed by voices off

BIBLE REFERENCE
Joshua 6

Abey Well, best of order please ladies and gentlemen as we come to item four on the agenda.

Seedee 'Bout time too.

Abey I beg your pardon.

Seedee Item four concerns the noise pollution from beyond the city wall caused by the *(spits)* Israelites.

Abey What is the nature of the complaint?

Seedee Are you deaf?

Abey Come, come Councillor Seedee, that's no way to treat the Chair. There's a certain formality to these proceedings you know.

Seedee Sorry my friend. I forgot myself for a moment. The noise has been particularly offensive. It breaks my concentration.

Abey Quite so, quite so. For the record then, please set out the nature of the complaint.

Seedee Well for the past six days a large crowd has been deliberately and provocatively marching round the outside of the city. They have been making extensive noise by stamping in an exaggerated manner the while.

Abey And furthermore…

Seedee And furthermore, Councillor Abey, contrary to subsection B (part 2) of the by-laws of the Greater Jericho Chamber of Corporate Affairs, they have this very morning commenced an escalation of marching beyond the one march per day practised earlier, this time sounding rams' horns.

Abey Rams' horns?

Seedee Indeed. They're a sort of trumpet.

Abey What sort of a trumpet?

Seedee A flippin' loud one.

The theme music from The Great Escape *comes from off-stage.*

Abey I think I can hear them now. That is very loud. Is someone shouting as well?

Seedee They are. They've started shouting. That is the last straw. I move that they are officially cautioned, bound over to keep silent, restrained from being within one mile of the city walls and the rams' horns be confiscated.

Abey Seems reasonable. All agreed?

Seedee What was that crashing sound?

STOP PRESS

Mac is sitting at his desk. Jez rushes in looking soaked to the skin and very bedraggled.

Mac Jez, Jez. What happened to you man?

Jez *(Words tumbling over each other)* I, I was just, I mean we were up on the mountain and, oh my god, the blood was terrible and it was pouring with rain and the fire wouldn't start and then fire like you'd never seen before and it was hot and it was awful and I just…

Mac Jez. Get a grip. You're my best reporter here. What's been going on?

Jez All the prophets of Baal are dead.

Mac All of them?

Jez All of them are dead, Mac. Slaughtered.

Mac Who did this, Jez?

Jez Elijah the prophet. Well no, Elijah the prophet's God actually. Well no, in fact the people did it. But Elijah made them.

Mac Jez. Pull yourself together. You don't know how stupid you sound. How on earth do you make people slaughter 400 prophets?

Jez Turn on the telly.

Mac What?

Jez Turn on the telly. *(Mac does so.)*

TV reporter The Wadi Kishon is a raging torrent from the heavy rain but still, above the water line, is evidence of a mass killing. Evidence of the ethnic cleansing instigated by the mad prophet Elijah, who is now reputed to be on the run, can

still be seen clearly. This is Iqbal, Sidonian National Television Service in the Kishon Valley, handing you back to the studio.

Mac Wow, Jez, some story! And you were there?

Jez Sure was.

Mac Find me Elijah.

Jez What?

Mac You heard.

Jez I heard. I just don't think I want to find him very much. If someone's just developed a reputation as an axe-murderer the last thing on their mind is going to be a newspaper interview.

Mac Jez, Jez. You're my best man. There's a huge story here. Get after it. Sooner or later this Elijah's going to do something else and I want you there when he does it. Meantime I'll put someone on this just breaking. *(Takes piece of paper off desk)* Apparently Horeb's had an earthquake, a fire and a hurricane all at the same time.

CAST
Mac (a newspaper editor), Jez (his reporter) and a TV reporter (optional)

SCENE
A newspaper office

PRODUCTION NOTES
The TV report can either be done by a taped voice, or by an actor with their head inside a dummy TV screen.

Props
• desk with papers on it
• a dummy TV screen

BIBLE REFERENCE
1 Kings 18:16-46

SAMARITANS

CAST
Samaritans telephone counsellor

SCENE
Telephone switchboard desk

PRODUCTION NOTES
The counsellor should pause between lines as if the other person was speaking.

Props
• a phone or hands-free device with headset

BIBLE REFERENCE
Job 1-42

Samaritan Good evening, Samaritans.

Hello?

You sound very distressed. Would you like to tell me what happened?

Your oxen and donkeys were stolen?

And your servants killed?

And your sheep were stolen?

And your camels were stolen?

And then you heard that all your sons and daughters had died in a terrible accident?

Hello? Are you still there?

Yes, of course. That is more than anyone could bear.

Thank you so much for asking me to listen to you. If you ever want to call again just do so.

Freeze and pause.

Samaritan Good evening, Samaritans.

Yes I do remember you, Job. All those appalling tragedies on the same day. How are things? You don't sound at all well.

What's been the trouble?

Oh that sounds awful. Is the rash really irritating?

Ouch! Oo, Job, that's so…

… scratching, scratching, scratching, scratching…

Oh, Job! Horrible!

It's really good that you felt you could call us. We're here for you anytime.

Freeze and pause.

Samaritan Good evening, Samaritans.

Hello again. How could I forget you, Job? Are you feeling any better?

I see. You've had some friends call round. That must have been a comfort to you.

Until they opened their mouths? Why? What did they say?

(After long pause) I see. No, I don't think it was good advice to laugh at destruction and famine. Is that all they said?

'One day your lips will shout with joy'? True, that won't make you feel any better now. What did your third friend say?

'You're a sinner.' Hmmm. Job, may I ask you how you feel about your friends now?

(After long pause) No, of course I don't think you're a maggot and a worm.

Well I'm delighted you called again. No, thank *you*.

Freeze and pause.

Samaritan Good evening, Samaritans.

Hello?

Job? Is that you? Job, I'm sure that's you. Can you speak to me? What's happened?

You didn't know what you were

talking about? How do you mean? Perhaps it would help to start at the beginning.

It's often the case. No, it doesn't surprise me that someone young should be helpful.

He's helped you to see God in his true perspective. Well that's good. But you're still obviously very distressed. What happened next? Can you talk about it?

No, Job, of course I understand. Maybe another time.

Freeze and pause.

Samaritan Good evening, Samaritans.

I'm sorry but this phone line is reserved for people in distress. If you want to laugh I suggest you call …

Job! Well my… I wouldn't have believed…

Well that's brilliant. But what about the rash?

Completely?

And you've had all your family round. Brilliant.

And they gave you money to replace your possessions? Fantastic.

Well, it's been an honour to talk to you Job. I don't always hear happy endings, but you seem to have got things worked out now. What was the turning point for you do you think?

When the Lord spoke to you out of a storm. I see. Well, good night Job. Good night.

Samaritan puts the phone down or indicates the call is over some other way.

You know, I can't understand how some people keep their faith in God.

9

PREGNANT PAUSE

CAST
Mary and a doctor's receptionist

SCENE
Doctor's surgery

PRODUCTION NOTES
Props
• a few blank forms

BIBLE REFERENCE
Luke 1:26-56

Receptionist Good morning. Can I help you?

Mary Yes. Er… I've not been here before, but I think I need to register to see a doctor.

Receptionist That's fine. There's just a few forms to fill in. Are you here because you're unwell?

Mary Yes; I mean, no… that is…

Receptionist (Interrupting) Surely that's a simple enough question? Either you're well or you're not well?

Mary (Trying to be more confident) I think I'm pregnant.

Receptionist I see. Gosh, you're very young to be married.

Mary I'm not married.

Receptionist What! Well you'd better learn to keep your voice down then. You know the penalty for that sort of thing.

Mary No, no, no, you don't understand. I haven't done anything wrong.

Receptionist You are young aren't you? If you were a bit older you'd know the penalty for unlawful sexual intercourse. This isn't Corinth. You can choose between abortion and death by stoning.

Mary But I haven't had unlawful sexual intercourse.

Receptionist Look. I don't want to have a row with you here, but you must know that there's only one way to become pregnant and that's to have sexual intercourse. If you're not married it's unlawful.

Mary (Quietly) There is another way. (To herself) My soul proclaims the greatness of the Lord and my spirit rejoices in God my Saviour.

Receptionist Pardon.

Mary I said, there is another way.

Receptionist Well tell me about it. I've always thought men were rather irrelevant and this could just about do away with them altogether.

Mary Couldn't I just see a doctor? I'd like to be sure.

Receptionist Yes but I'd love to know about the 'other way'.

Mary Well there was an angel. And he said the Holy Spirit would come upon me and I would be with child. From now on all generations will call me blessed.

Receptionist laughs heartily.

Mary He did. He did.

Receptionist Don't you know who the father is?

Mary Oh I'm sure about the identity of the father.

Receptionist Come on. Come on. Is the father much older than you?

Mary (Very long pause and mental torment) I think so.

Receptionist I think you've come to the wrong clinic my love. I'll just phone the mental health unit and see who's on duty. Won't be a minute. (Calls out) Zechariah and Elizabeth, the doctor will see you now.

REALMS OF GLORY

Michael and Gabriel are on stage. Michael walks to centre-stage and jumps backwards, making a sucking noise.

Gabriel Thhhtoomm! (*He then repeats the process two or three times.*)

Michael (*Who has been watching*) What in heaven are you doing, your Grace?

Gabriel Practising, Excellency.

Michael Practising what, your Honour?

Gabriel De-manifesting, my Lord.

Michael But Gabriel, you've done that hundreds of times. Didn't you win the 'Best Exit' award in the 'Herald of the Year' bash a few years back? You don't get one of those without being able to de-manifest properly.

Gabriel Quite so, Michael my brother. But that was in a large open space. It's easy to exit spectacularly with a bit of dust and cloud if you de-manifest in the middle of a field. This particular de-manifest has to happen in a confined space.

Michael Glory, laud and honour! That is awkward. A split second out and you can block the gates of heaven with some poor chap's furniture. I understand your predicament. Is there a human in the room?

Gabriel There is.

Michael De-manifest too suddenly and you'll suck out his eardrums. Like Cyril did. They haven't let him go back since, except the next day for the healing. Where have you got to go?

Gabriel The holy of holies in the temple of the Lord, Sire.

CAST
Two angels – we'll call them Michael and Gabriel

SCENE
Heaven or somewhere

PRODUCTION NOTES
Any costumes or props should show the great eminence of these angels. Avoid silly wings and the rest.

BIBLE REFERENCE
Luke 1:5-25; 2:8-20

Michael (*Sucks his breath in sharply*) Whew!

Gabriel Next to the incense supply.

Michael So you can't come in at altitude and fly down like normal?

Gabriel No, but I've got the hang of manifesting. I've got the coordinates down to five decimal places. I've built a dummy planet with a temple and everything. The budget on this one is virtually infinite. I can manifest into a room without even blowing out the candles.

Michael That is impressive.

Gabriel Yes. The first time I blew out the door, melted all the candles and would have boiled a human being if there'd been one.

Michael Did it take long to get it right?

Gabriel Only two hundred years. It was nowhere near as difficult as learning to do those stone tablets without so much as singeing his beard. And I've got a speech to learn too. (*Pushes shoulders back and delivers soliloquy*) 'Do not be afraid, Zechariah; your prayer has been heard. Your wife Elizabeth will bear you a son…'

Michael (*Laughing*) 'Do not be afraid!' If he knew how close he was about to come to entering the kingdom of heaven through the extractor unit he'd be speechless.

Gabriel He's going to be speechless if he asks any questions.

Michael Oh the poor so and so. Struck dumb for lack of faith if he so much as blinks? Has the Master really deemed this one so important?

Gabriel He certainly has, O Great One. But enough of me.

How's your preparation going?

Michael Oh the singing's going great. The sound of four thousand angels singing 'Glory to God in the Highest' in fifteen part harmony is truly wonderful.

Gabriel So what's the problem, your Worship?

Michael The problem is getting them into formation at 20,000 feet having come in on the beacon coordinates. We've been practising over some hills in Australia. We can now manifest in with only a few ruffled feathers and the sound of distant thunder. We were doing all right until we tried it in the dark.

Gabriel So who's benefit is it all for?

Michael Some shepherds.

Gabriel Sounds important. What's a shepherd?

Michael I don't know, but the Master has a soft spot for them.

Gabriel Well at least you've got four hundred years to get this right.

Michael Indeed. But from what I hear the next one is going to be even worse. *All* the equipment's booked out for the finale.

ORANGES ARE THE ONLY FRUIT

Preacher Well, good afternoon (morning, evening) everybody and welcome to.................... *(church name)*. Our Christingle service begins with carol number .... *(details of carol)*.

Heckler *(Entering with a commotion)* Hang on a minute. *(Stomping up centre aisle)* What on earth are you doing?

Preacher *(Patiently)* Please make yourself at home. We're just about to start our Christingle service with a carol.

Heckler Christingle service?

Preacher Yes. Please sit down.

Heckler *(Goes to sit then stands again)* But look at all these poor, defenceless oranges.

Preacher Are you serious?

Heckler Never more so. How would you like it if someone took you away from your primary purpose, made a whopping great hole in you and stuck a candle in the hole…

Preacher *(Interrupting)* Well I…

Heckler *(Carrying on regardless)*… then stuck four cocktail sticks into you and tied a piece of ribbon around your bum as if that made everything all right. *(Starting to rant)* Free the Citric Seven. Justice and a fair deal for Christmas fruit. We demand parity with satsumas and clementines. 'The future's bright.' Not for oranges round here it isn't pal.

Preacher You're missing the point. We're not torturing innocent oranges; we're using them to symbolize a far deeper truth.

Heckler Can't you use kiwi fruits? Nobody likes them.

Preacher No we can't. Oranges symbolize the world God has created. They're bright and they're round.

Heckler And the candle?

Preacher Jesus, the light of the world.

Heckler So perhaps we can do without the sticks. They must hurt.

Preacher I don't want to argue with you about the feelings of oranges – *(aside)* I don't think I'd get very far – but the sticks and the fruit and nuts represent the four seasons and God's provision of food.

Heckler The ribbon?

Preacher The blood of Jesus Christ, shed for the sins of the world.

Heckler That sounds a bit cruel.

Preacher Well it was quite horrible; but it was God's idea. These oranges – we call them Christingles – have a much deeper meaning than you would expect.

Heckler I still think it's all rather unfair, but can I stay and listen to the rest of the service?

Preacher Of course. Why not sit down. *(Heckler does so this time.)* We'll now start our Christingle Service by singing.......................... *(details of carol)*. Please stand.

CAST
A preacher and a heckler

SCENE
The front of church

PRODUCTION NOTES
This is designed to make the opening of a Christingle service more interesting. The Christingles should be displayed prominently on a table at the front of church.

Props
• a placard saying 'Stick your sticks elsewhere' or some such nonsense

BREADLINE

CAST
Narrator 1, Narrator 2,
John and John's mum

SCENE
John's house

PRODUCTION NOTES
The narrators stand at either side of the stage. John and his mum mime.

BIBLE REFERENCE
Mark 6:30-44

Narrator 1 John got back from the day out.

Enter John

Narrator 2 He was tired…

John yawns.

Narrator 1 Very tired.

He nods off.

Narrator 1 Very tired and hungry…

John shakes his head and holds his stomach as if stuffed full.

Narrator 2 Er, excuse me!

Narrator 1 What is it? I'm narrating here.

Narrator 2 He wasn't hungry.

Narrator 1 Had to be mate. Had to be. He only had some bread and fish all day. Have you seen his mum's packed lunches?

Enter Mum, looking angrily at narrator.

Narrator 2 She may be Mrs Mean's meaner older sister, but he's not hungry.

Mum continues to look daggers at both narrators now, whilst John sits down.

Narrator 1 What happened? Someone feed him extra for nothing did they?

John nods. Mum starts getting cross with him and wagging finger.

Narrator 2 Something like that, yes. He met a man you see.

Narrator 1 His mum's going to go ballistic. He hasn't been accepting food off strangers has he?

Mum goes ballistic(ish).

Narrator 2 Well they don't come any stranger, but he hasn't been harmed has he? And he's brought some extra food home.

Mum cheers up.

Narrator 1 Extra food? How much?

Narrator 2 Oh quite a lot.

Narrator 1 How much is 'quite a lot'.

Narrator 2 How many baskets John?

John mimes twelve using ten fingers, then two.

Narrator 1 Well that will keep the wolf from the door.

Narrator 2 Actually, I think they ate the wolf.

Narrator 1 Twelve baskets of left-overs. That's a result.

Mum and John hug each other.

PLANKS

The two Christians enter with planks of wood strapped to their heads.

One Morning.

Two All right?

One How are you?

Two I'm fine, actually.

One Really!

Two Excuse me?

One Oh, nothing.

Two No, what is it?

One It's nothing that you don't know already.

Two And what do you mean by that?

One You tell me!

Two I'll…

One Yes, so I've heard!

Two I'm…

One I've heard that, too; you should pray harder. But tell me, how is the vicar?

Two She's fine…

One I *bet* she is!

Two What…

One It's all round town, you know. Everyone's talking about it. I don't know how you've managed to keep it a secret. I almost admire you. Almost…

Two I have no idea what you're talking about.

One Of course you don't. And you've probably forgotten that you've been to visit her twice already this week, haven't you?

Two Errr… no.

One And that you were both seen in old Bill's field last week.

Two *(Raises eyebrows)*

One And that you've been having an affair for the last six months!

CAST
Two Christians (One and Two), Jesus

SCENE
Anywhere

PRODUCTION NOTES
Props
• two planks and some clever way of strapping them to the actors' heads
• a saw
• Jesus wears a T-shirt with 'Jesus' on it, preferably written rather clumsily in felt-tip

BIBLE REFERENCE
Matthew 7:1-5

Two WHAT?

One So you don't deny it then?

Two There's nothing to deny.

One You're bound to say that.

Two We're *not* having an affair.

One And that.

Two (*Short pause*) Where did you hear this?

One That would be telling… but someone heard you talking to her last week outside her house. Someone heard you say that you were having an affair and that it wasn't easy.

Two That's rubbish! When did you hear this?

One Last Tuesday.

Two Well, whoever overheard me got it wrong.

One Oh, isn't that convenient?

Two Well, yes. Especially when I actually said we were planning a fair and that it wasn't easy. You know; the church fair. The one held every year in Bill's field. The one that is flooded at the moment.

One (*Disappointed*) Oh.

Two Oh! Is that all you can say? Especially after…

One After what?

Two After that business at the pet shop.

One What business at the pet shop?

Jesus enters carrying a saw.

Jesus Excuse me?

One & Two WHAT?

Jesus You'll be needing this. (*He hands over the saw.*)

One What are you? A carpenter or something?

All freeze.

PERSISTENCE

Harriet Sborin' today init?

Henrietta Very. I used ter think life would be easier without the customers, but I tell you what, I'm gaggin' for that line to get hot again.

Harriet People just don't seem ter 'ave any enthusiasm for prayer these days.

Henrietta Say what. Time was there was a constant stream of callers. Urgent, non-urgent, regulars…

Harriet Have you had yer 'air dun then?

Henrietta Wha?

Harriet Looks different.

Henrietta Couldn't 'ave dried it properly.

The telephone rings. Harriet picks it up but says nothing.

Henrietta 'Oo is it?

Harriet (*Covering receiver for this and all subsequent lines*) It's 'er.

Henrietta 'Oo?

Harriet 'Er. (*These last two lines should come out as 'oo-er'.*)

Henrietta 'Asn't she got justice yet?

Harriet 'Parently not.

Henrietta Well in't it 'bout time? (*Harriet mimics someone who just keeps talking.*) She's very persistent in't she?

Harriet I think that's the point.

Henrietta Whadder yer mean?

Harriet I mean we don't get many callers 'oo are 'appy to keep calling 'gain 'n' again 'n' again even though we never say anyfink.

Henrietta But that's the point init?

Harriet Well I nevva got told that in staff training.

Henrietta Well you should 'ave been.

Harriet If that's true then all that gets changed by praying is the person what prays.

Henrietta So?

Harriet So that's unfair.

Henrietta Well what you goin' to do 'bout it?

Harriet (*Putting phone down as if she doesn't care about the caller*) I'm goin' to move the file up the queue.

Henrietta What queue?

Harriet Any queue. Just as long as she don't phone again.

Henrietta You can't do that.

Harriet I can. And I'm going to do this. (*She takes a marker pen and writes 'ERGUNT' on the folder in big letters.*)

Henrietta I can't see that 'elping.

Harriet I've gotta do something. She's wearing me out.

They freeze.

CAST
Harriet and Henrietta (the staff of the angelic prayer line)

SCENE
An office in heaven (use your imagination)

PRODUCTION NOTES
Ideally, someone should read Luke 18:1-8 at the end of the sketch as the actors remain frozen.

Props
• two clipboards
• a desk with a large telephone on it
• an empty light-coloured envelope folder
• a marker pen

FX
• a telephone ringing (taped or the real thing)

BIBLE REFERENCE
Luke 18:1-8

100 PER CENT VISUALLY IMPAIRED

CAST
Farrah See (a TV presenter), Darkus Night (a healed man) and Dimas (his mum)

SCENE
A breakfast TV studio

PRODUCTION NOTES
Props
• these can be low-key (just a sofa) or over the top with lights, cameras and extra actors

FX
• cringey breakfast-TV music as an opening theme creates an appropriate atmosphere

BIBLE REFERENCE
John 9

Farrah Well, good morning world and welcome back to *Early Morning.* We're going to hear a remarkable story now. Until last week Darkus Night was unable to see anything at all. Indeed he has been unable to see since birth. But now, following a remarkable encounter, his eyesight appears to be fully restored. Well, let's hear the story because he's here this morning. Welcome to *Early Morning,* and come in please, Darkus Night. *(Darkus enters to applause and cheers.)* Darkus, thanks for agreeing to come on the show. Now until last week I think I'm correct in saying you were 100 per cent visually impaired?

Darkus I was blind, yes.

Farrah So what happened?

Darkus Well I was selling *Big Issue* at my usual pitch when this gang came along. They weren't locals as far as I could tell. And they were talking about blindness.

Farrah What were they saying?

Darkus Well they seemed to be discussing whether I had done something to deserve to be blind or not.

Farrah Then what happened?

Darkus Then one of them – he seemed to be the leader – covered my eyes in some horrible, gunky stuff – someone told me had spat in it – and so I went off to wash my face. He said to go to the pool down the street, which made sense because it was the nearest place.

Farrah Disgusting. How did you feel?

Darkus Furious. I was going to lose sales; might even lose my pitch.

Farrah So you washed?

Darkus Yeah, I washed, and when I splashed the water on my eyes I washed my eyesight on. I could see. I was so amazed I went home and left all me mags on the street corner.

Farrah So what do you know about the guy who did this?

Darkus I don't know him.

Farrah And how did he manage to heal your eyes?

Darkus No idea.

Farrah Well, let's bring on another guest at this point. Please welcome Darkus's mum, Mrs Night. Come in Dimas. *(Dimas enters to applause.)* Mrs Night, has your son always been blind?

Dimas Yes.

Farrah And he's had doctors look at his eyes?

Dimas We're not a wealthy family. When Darkus was born we were told he was blind and we had to cope. He's a good boy.

Farrah So how come he can see now?

Dimas Young lady, if I knew that I'd be out doin' healings meself.

Farrah So tell us again, Darkus: how did the man get your eyes to work?

Darkus Don't you listen? We don't know.

18

Farrah Were you really blind Darkus, or were you just a stooge for that guy?

Darkus Are you calling me a cheat?

Farrah I'm simply voicing concern on behalf of our viewers. Some people say you're not the man who was blind; you just look like him. Is that true?

Darkus I don't know what *I* looked like last week, let alone anyone else.

Farrah We've spoken to your doctor and he says you were never officially registered as blind. Indeed, if you had been you could have claimed financial help.

Darkus Look, all I know is that last week I couldn't see and this week I can. Why should I answer all your questions? Go and find the guy who did it.

Farrah We will. We will.

Dimas Maybe he'll open your eyes too. You ought to show some respect, young lady. We're not staying here. Come on Darkus. *(They stomp off set.)*

Farrah *(Slightly flustered)* And on that note we'll take a break. Next on *Early Morning*, a man who claims he used to be dead. Back in three minutes. Don't leave the table.

IT'S CURTAINS FOR JESUS

Sam sits at a desk. Nat walks in looking troubled.

Sam Hi. It's Nat er, er… *(grasping for name)* Templeman. Haven't seen you since the tables and doves claim. Come to pay your premium?

Nat No Sam, premium's not due for another couple of months. I'm afraid I need another claim form.

Sam Another claim Nat? You're going to lose your bonus year at this rate. What is it this time?

Nat A curtain.

Sam Only a curtain? That's not exactly going to wreck your claims experience. The look on your face I thought you were going to tell me the whole temple needed rebuilding.

Nat *(Scathingly and almost interrupting)* That's not a joking matter.

Sam Oops, sorry! No need to be touchy. Let's just get the form filled in, shall we? *(He takes a claim form from his drawer.)* Now then, you said it was a curtain. What was the nature of the damage?

Nat It was ripped.

Sam And when did this happen?

Nat Friday, middle of the afternoon.

Sam And how did it happen? *(He looks up. Nat shakes his head resignedly.)* Well?

Nat Sam, I don't know how it happened. It looks like vandalism, but what vandal climbs to the top of a curtain and rips it from the top to the bottom?

Sam And the value?

Nat Priceless.

Sam Nat, which curtain are we talking about exactly?

Nat The curtain which excludes the impure from the holy of holies.

Sam That is going to spoil your claims experience. That's a big curtain. It wasn't that guy again was it? You know; the one who caused all the damage to those nice tables and let the pigeons out?

Nat No, he's got an alibi. It couldn't have been him.

Sam What happened to him? Twenty lashes? Forty?

Nat We crucified him on Friday.

Sam Gee! *(Exhales sharply)* That's a bit harsh isn't it? Still it's a good alibi. *(Pauses)* What are we going to put down as cause of damage?

Nat Can't you just put it down as an accident?

Sam *(A bit sarcastically)* Oh that'll look fine won't it? 'Accidentally ripped a forty-foot curtain from top to bottom.'

Nat Sam. Help me. I'm struggling here. There's been some strange things going on the last few days. I know what I think, but I can hardly find it in me to say the words.

Sam I wouldn't bother saying it here. Specific exclusion on all policies issued from this office. You can't make a claim for an act of God.

Both freeze.

RISING

The Sadducee and the body are both on stage.

Sadducee I am a Sadducee. I do not believe in the resurrection of the dead.

A telephone rings, off-stage. After two rings, an answerphone message cuts in and the voice of the dead body is heard.

Body *(Playback of recording)* Hello. I'm sorry I can't take your call right now as I'm dead. If you want to leave a message after the tone I'll get back to you should something unexpected happen.

Sadducee I'm sitting here thinking about what I just said because there is a man going around saying that he is the resurrection and the life. Bit controversial that. I thought if I sat next to a tomb I might get a better perspective on the matter. *(He wafts his hand in front of his nose.)* Bit wiffy though; don't half stink.

Voice 1 Lazarus! Come out!

The body gets up and walks off, taking the tiny steps of a man whose feet are bandaged together.

Sadducee I don't believe it!

Voice 2 *(In best BBC English)* Thank you for calling the BT answering service. You have forty-seven outstanding messages.

Body I don't believe it!

CAST
A Sadducee, a dead body and two voices off

SCENE
Some sort of tomb

PRODUCTION NOTES
The body's first speech should be pre-recorded. The other two telephone voices are most effective if pre-recorded, but can be performed by off-stage actors. The body should be wrapped in a roll of toilet paper.

Props
• a roll of toilet paper

BIBLE REFERENCE
John 11:1-44

EVANGELISM TRAINING

CAST
Peter, Lucinda and Seb
(all disciples)

SCENE
A room in Jerusalem

PRODUCTION NOTES
Props
• a lectern

(This sketch is influenced by Nick Revill and Andy Hamilton's 'Pirate Sketch' from *The Million Pound Radio Show*, BBC Radio 4.)

BIBLE REFERENCE
Acts 1:8

Peter stands behind a lectern. The other two are listening intently.

Peter *(As if caught in mid-sentence)* … and to Samaria and to the ends of the earth. Friends, that is the mission the Lord has given us. Let's go!

Lucinda Where?

Peter Into the streets of Jerusalem to spread the good news.

Lucinda Isn't that a bit hasty?

Seb Yeah. What about a plan?

Peter A plan? Lucinda. Sebastian. We've got a mission to the ends of the earth starting in Jerusalem. What more of a plan do you need?

Seb A five-year plan.

Lucinda A mission statement.

Seb We need to start with some focus groups.

Lucinda And some role-play.

Peter Role-play? The people out there don't know the good news of Jesus raised from the dead. We need to offer eternal life, urgently.

Seb You haven't briefed us yet.

Lucinda Give us a workbook.

Seb Handouts.

Lucinda I don't think any of us have even seen the video yet.

Peter Video? We can't sit around waiting for two thousand years for video to be invented. There's thousands of people in Jerusalem and we have to do Judea and the ends of the earth as well. We need to start.

Seb What's our daily target?

Lucinda Is this piece work?

Seb What about overtime?

Lucinda Bonuses?

Peter Look. We're disciples. And disciples don't need any incentive save that of doing the Master's will. We will strive to spread the good news despite floggings, imprisonment, insults, mocking and eventually will lay down our lives in his service.

Seb Well that's hardly going to motivate us now is it?

Lucinda Give us a correspondence course.

Seb Send us to a spiritual director.

Lucinda We ought to pray about it, you know.

Seb Yes. And we haven't got a budget.

Peter *(Totally charismatic leadership)* Look. We're disciples. So in a minute we're going to walk right out that door.

Lucinda and Seb *(Echoing)* Out that door.

Peter We're going to go right up to the first strangers we see.

Lucinda and Seb First strangers we see.

Peter We're going to introduce ourselves.

Lucinda and Seb Introduce ourselves.

Peter And take up a collection for missionary work.

SONGS OF PRAISE

Disciple 2 stands centre stage.

Disciple 1 *(Enters, holding letter)*
'I will enter his gates with thanksgiving in my heart,
I will enter his courts with praise;
da da da da, I will say…'[1]

Disciple 2 *(Interrupting)*
Someone's cheerful today.

Disciple 1 'There's no other way…'[2] *(Waves letter)*

Disciple 2 What's that?

Disciple 1 'He speaks and
li-i-i-i-istening to-oo hi-is voice,
New life the dead receive,
New li-i-i-i-ife the dead receive…'[3]

Disciple 2 Heavy. It's not from Paul is it?

Disciple 1 '… for there is no other name…'[4]

Disciple 2 Let me see that. *(Snatches letter and reads from it)* 'Put on the full armour of God so that you can take your stand against the devil's schemes.'

Disciple 1 '… higher…'[5]

Disciple 2 *(Looking higher up the page)* 'Speak to one another with psalms, hymns and spiritual songs. Sing and make music in your heart to the Lord.' So that's the cause of all this?

Disciple 1 'Now thank we all our God,
With hearts, and hands, and voices…'[6]

Disciple 2 I don't think Paul means you can *only* speak in songs. At least if he does you're going to have a job persuading people to pass you the cornflakes in the morning.

Disciple 1 'Where things impossible by faith shall be made possible…'[7]

Disciple 2 Look, *(waves letter back)* a bit further down it says 'And pray in the Spirit on all occasions with all kinds of prayers and requests. With this in mind, be alert and always keep on praying for all the saints.' You can't sing *and* pray *all* the time.

Disciple 1 'He turns our weaknesses into his opportunities…'[8]

Disciple 2 What about those of us who can't sing?

Disciple 1 'Hark! how the heavenly anthem drowns,
All music but its own…'[9]

Disciple 2 I don't think you'll end up with many friends if you keep doing this.

Disciple 1 'When the fear of loneliness is looming,
Then remember I am at your side…'[10]

Disciple 2 Suit yourself. *(Exits, clutching letter)*

Disciple 1 'Climb every mountain,
Ford every stream…'[11]

Disciple 2 *(Shouting from off stage)* And I think you'd better do some more research on that one.

CAST
Two disciples, one of whom can sing a bit

SCENE
Anywhere

PRODUCTION NOTES
All the lines by Disciple 1 are sung. At the foot of the page there is a list of the songs quoted. You could adapt the sketch to use other songs well-known in your setting.

Props
• a very long letter

BIBLE REFERENCE
Ephesians 5:19

1. 'I will enter his gates with thanksgiving in my heart', Leona van Brethorst © 1976 Maranatha! Music USA.
2. 'How can I be free from sin' (Lead me to the cross), Kendrick & Thompson © 1991 Make Way Music.
3. 'O for a thousand tongues', Charles Wesley.
4. 'There is power in the name of Jesus', Noel Richards © 1989 Kingsway's Thankyou Music.
5. As 4.
6. 'Now thank we all our God', Martin Rinkart.
7. 'Rejoice, rejoice', Graham Kendrick © 1983 Kingsway's Thankyou Music.
8. As 7.
9. 'Crown him with many crowns', Matthew Bridges.
10. 'Do not be afraid', Gerald Markland © 1978 Kevin Mayhew Ltd.
11. 'Climb every mountain' from *The Sound of Music*.

PUB SKETCH 1: HOLY SPIRIT AT CONFIRMATION

CAST
Steve and Bob (two members of the church drama group), a bartender and a posse of voices off

SCENE
A pub

PRODUCTION NOTES
In-depth study has shown that a single can of Boddingtons will produce sufficient brown liquid to part-fill two glasses. Method actors may require more in order to get into role. The two drama group members should be of the same gender.

Props
• at least four glasses
• some beer
• a tea towel
• a bar (perhaps a covered table)

Steve What's the vicar asked us to do this time?

Bob Well, we've got to write a sketch for the confirmation service.

Steve What is the question we want the drama to leave in people's minds?

Bob Well I suppose it's 'What is the efficacy of the Holy Spirit at confirmation?'

Steve The what-icacy?

Bob Efficacy!

Bartender Mind your language please!

Pause.

Steve So what's the answer? Do we need to talk about tongues of fire and rushing wind and a huge injection of life and love and the bishop's cassock being blown up into the air…

Bob *(Interrupting)* Come on; be serious. *(Pause)* You were confirmed. What's the answer?

Steve It was a long time ago. Anyway, you've got a theology degree. You should know.

Bob It doesn't make any difference to me. I'm a Baptist.

Bartender So what are you two talking about this time?

(They look at each other and shrug.)

Steve *(Resigned)* We are discussing 'What is the efficacy of the Holy Spirit at confirmation?'

Bartender Wholly spirit? 100 per cent? You'd kill people.

Bob No, Holy Spirit. 'Holy' as in 'separate, apart, pure'. It's the person of God who enters into a believer's life at…

Steve Confirmation!

Bob No, baptism.

Steve Let's say 'conversion'.

Bob Er, no, let's just say 'It's the person of God who indwells a believer.'

Bartender What's confirmation?

Steve It's a service at which Christians confirm their baptism vows…

Bob … and the church confirms their membership…

Steve … and the bishop asks God to confirm with his Holy Spirit.

Bartender So what's efforty-thingy?

Steve & Bob *(Together)* Efficacy!

Voices off *(Shouting)* Mind your language!

Bob It's the effect. It's about what actually happens and does it change anything.

Bartender Can't you give me an ordinary example?

Steve You see that certificate on the wall?

Bartender What, the Cellar Keeper's Hygiene Certificate that says I'm qualified to keep good beer.

Steve Yeah! What's the efficacy of that?

Bartender *(Vehemently)* Doesn't have any efficacy at all. It's just a piece of paper. I could keep beer long before I went on that course. Some of the geezers on the course couldn't keep disinfectant. It takes years. It takes experience.

Bob So there is no efficacy to that piece of paper. The brewery are wasting their time having certification at all?

Bartender *(Even more vehemently)* Don't be stupid. You can't just let anybody keep beer. Not untrained people. 'Scuse me; someone wants serving. *(Wanders off)*

Bob *(Sighs)* So what is the efficacy of the Holy Spirit at confirmation?

Steve I don't know. But that is the question.

Pause

Bob I'd like to test the efficacy of that certificate some more.

Steve OK. We can write the sketch while we're doing it.

THE AFTER-CHURCH INTERVIEW

CAST
Reverend Jones (a vicar)
and John Motson (a
football commentator)

SCENE
The back of church

PRODUCTION NOTES
Props
• a microphone

Motson Well, Reverend Jones, it's the end of another Sunday. How do you think it went?

Vicar Well, as I say, the lads done well and looked very well organized. Lots of discipline.

Motson You looked very good at the back, but some might say you lacked width and there was nothing up front to speak of.

Vicar Yeah, we were tight at the back but we've had trouble getting bodies forward for a few seasons now and today was no exception.

Motson And width? You could do with some movement out wide.

Vicar Yes, the side aisles are hard to fill but we have lots of commitment in the middle.

Motson How about the gate receipts today?

Vicar Yes, very pleasing, we packed a lot into the box. Our folk give everything they've got; not just ten per cent.

Motson Some might say that your stadium is very plain. Any plans to improve things there?

Vicar Well, we have been aware for some time that we're not getting enough crosses in and our corners are very disappointing.

Motson You seem to have fantastic support for a relatively small club and they make a lot of noise.

Vicar The team obviously means a lot to the community and we can get the crowds in for the big games. Come carols by candlelight and they'll be queuing three deep back round the block.

Motson That gives you problems?

Vicar Well naturally we would prefer to sell a few more season tickets. At the moment I'm more of an odd-job man than a manager.

Motson Your young preacher shows signs of real class. Looked very dangerous in the pulpit.

Vicar He's learning his trade really well. Plays it by the book but often leaves the opposition wondering which way he's going to go.

Motson And the one chance that came his way – never any doubt about that one was there?

Vicar Lovely finish. A real fisher of men who puts them in the back of the net. Give him the right service and he'll score as often as not.

Motson What about ego? It seems like one in three persons here think they're God.

Vicar Traditional belief has never been a problem for us.

Motson Holy Communion? Haven't seen that here yet?

Vicar True. We've not had a good run with the cup recently.

Motson But a lovely manoeuvre at the end.

Vicar Yes, the big lad in the centre picked up that beautifully weighted cross and went straight through the middle.

Motson Well, Reverend Jones, thank you very much. All the best for next week.

Vicar Thank you.

CHANGING THE BARRELS

Punter Evening, vicar.

Vicar Evening. What can I get you?

Punter What's on special?

Vicar Well, we've got a couple of very nice barrels on at the moment: Old Church Organ, which is marvellous – a really dark pint – fruity character with a hint of musty hymn book and a sense of time standing still…

Punter Getting enthusiastic in your old age!

Vicar Ah, yes, but the next is one of my favourites. It's a guest ale this one: Pete's Olde Pew-warmer.

Punter Great name!

Vicar Too right, and it's fantastic! It's served chilled and combines an initial flatness with a tingly after-taste. Marvellous stuff!

Punter Hmmm…

Vicar There's the usuals as well, obviously: Cranmer's 1662, Old Coffee Morning, Summer Holiday Club, Old Incomprehensible…

Punter What's that?

Vicar It's just 1662 but I water it down a bit.

Punter I'll have a pint of Olde Pew-warmer please, and a hymn sandwich, if you've got any. (*Vicar pours pint and fetches sandwich. Punter sips pint.*) That's better. (*As he bites the sandwich, there is the sound of a hymn being sung.*) Not so busy tonight, then?

Vicar 'Fraid not, but that's the way it is nowadays, isn't it? I'm used to it.

Punter I guess. Don't know why people want those new family pubs, though. Me? I prefer a bit of the old traditional stuff.

Vicar So do I, so do I. I mean, what's wrong with this place? We've been here for years, serving the community, providing. We've got traditional ales, timeless tunes… What more could you want?

Punter Nothing! Pubs aren't meant to be full of kids for a start and as for that modern music…

Vicar Spoils the atmosphere!

Punter Exactly!

Vicar How's the beer?

Punter Lovely! Sits uncomfortably on the tongue and then surprises you with that tingle! The sandwich is nice, too. (*Takes a bite; the hymn is briefly louder.*)

Vicar None of that new fancy stuff here! It's all garnish now. Little extras, fancy tastes, special meats… I say 'stick with what you know'.

27

Punter Absolutely. What's the dressing?

Vicar Oh, just a bit of theology to give it some zing.

Punter Have you seen that new pub down the road?

Vicar Don't even start on that. I'm sick of it already. It's not been there long and already they're extending.

Punter Tell me about it! I live next door.

Vicar I know. And the noise…

Punter That's not the half of it. Inside they've got carpets, comfy seats, modern music, tea and coffee…

Vicar Tea and coffee! We're PUBS, not CAFÉS! I saw their delivery yesterday.

Punter And?

Vicar Oh, well, they're into all those new foreign beers.

Punter What, that American stuff?

Vicar Yupp!

Punter German and Swiss theological fizz?

Vicar Have you even tasted them? There's nothing to them. All so refreshing and clean and attractively bottled. And the names…

Punter 'Guiltless'.

Vicar 'Wiser'.

Punter And they have dancing. Get drunk! In a pub! Disgusting.

Vicar I tell you, we're at risk. If this country's not careful it'll lose one of its greatest treasures, one of its longest standing institutions; something that used to be the centre of every community.

Punter What are you going to do about it?

Vicar Well it's risky; but I'm going to play a hunch.

Punter And?

Vicar I'm going to guess that these newfangled places will go out of fashion and our customers will eventually come back.

Punter Wow, risky.

Vicar Yeah. Want a top up?

JUST THE FACTS

Newcomer Excuse me.

Minister Hello there.

Newcomer I was just wondering…

Minister Always welcome round here. We love wonderers.

Newcomer Er, quite. I was just wondering what you believed here.

Minister Come again?

Newcomer What is it you Christians believe?

Minister We are a community of faith.

Newcomer Could you be more specific?

Minister We are pilgrims on a journey towards the kingdom.

Newcomer Could you manage less cliché and more content?

Minister Well we believe we're saved by the blood of the Lamb.

Newcomer Could tell me with a little less metaphor?

Minister Well, our sins, though as scarlet, are washed as white as snow.

Newcomer And without simile?

Minister A carpenter from Nazareth needed joiners.

Newcomer OK. Once more without the pun please.

Minister For God so *loved* the *world*, that he gave his only begotten Son, that whosoever believeth in him should not perish, but have everlasting life.

Newcomer I think I've heard that before. Is it official?

Minister Yes, it's fully Authorized.

Newcomer Great. What does it mean?

Minister It means that *God* so *loved* the *world* that he gave his Son so that anyone who puts saving faith in his name should inherit life eternal.

Newcomer I think you've said that already. What does it mean?

Minister We can have life forever.

Newcomer Oxymoron.

Minister We're saved.

Newcomer Cliché.

Minister The power of prayer produces perfect peace.

Newcomer Is a little less alliteration available?

Minister But it's all a very sacred and holy mystery.

Newcomer Look will you tell me what you believe or I'm going to give you a good smack.

Minister Where will *that* get you?

Newcomer I've no idea, but I'll feel a lot better.

Minister Look why don't you just grab an ASB and an NIV?

Newcomer Where will that get me?

Minister C of E.

CAST
A minister and a newcomer

SCENE
The church door

PRODUCTION NOTES
This sketch would be ideal at the beginning of an evangelistic service if followed up by a punchy talk explaining what Christians do believe. The dialogue should be quick-fire, developing a sense of acceleration as the lines get shorter.

29

PUB SKETCH 2: WHAT IS HOLY COMMUNION?

Steve What's the vicar asked us to do this time?

Bob Well, we've got to write a sketch for Sunday's all-age service.

Steve What's it to be about?

Bob Holy Communion.

Steve What is the question we want the drama to leave in people's minds?

Bob I guess it's 'What does Holy Communion signify?' or 'What does Jesus mean by "Eat this in remembrance of me" or "He who drinks my blood"?'

Barman (*Pops up behind the bar*) What are you two talking about today?

Steve Excuse me, but why are you dressed as Batman?

Barman It was a misprint. I'm the barman. What are you two talking about?

Bob Holy Communion.

Barman Communion wine's dreadful. I've a nice case of Rioja I need to shift. Do you a good price.

Steve No, we're not planning a Communion; we're writing a sketch about what it means.

Barman What do you mean 'what does it mean?'? Why would someone be at a Holy Communion if they didn't know what it means? Strikes me the only people you'd expect to be there are people who know what it means.

Bob That's brilliant that.

Barman It is?

Bob Yeah. Brilliant. You wouldn't go to the opera if you didn't know what opera was, would you?

Steve I hate opera.

Bob So you don't go.

Steve Well actually I do. My wife likes it.

Bob Mmmmm… Why do people come to a pub?

Barman I have to. They pay me.

Bob Yeah *you* do. It's probably why the vicar goes to Communion.

Steve But why do ordinary people go there?

Barman It's like sex isn't it?

Steve & Bob (*Together and loudly*) What?

Barman Going to the pub. (*Steve and Bob shrug.*) You come here. There is an exchange of Boddington fluids with the brewery. You give money.

Bob That's nothing like sex.

Barman You're entitled to your opinion. You imbibe the result of their craft and become part of the community of sad, inebriated souls called 'regulars'. Excuse me. I see another lost soul in need of my tender mercy. (*Exits*)

Steve So where were we when we were interrupted?

Bob I dunno. What does 'drink my blood' mean?

Barman (*Shouted from off stage*) Case of Rioja anybody?

PUB SKETCH 3: THE TRINITY

The bartender stands behind the bar, drying a glass with a tea towel.

Steve What's the vicar asked us to do this time?

Bob Well, we've got to write a sketch about the Trinity.

Steve What is the question we want the drama to leave in people's minds?

Bob I suppose it's 'Why is the Christian faith best understood as Trinitarian?'

Steve And why is the Christian faith best understood as Trinitarian? Isn't it intrinsically monotheistic?

Bob Ah yes. If you read the Old Testament.

Steve I usually read the New Testament.

Bartender What are you two talking about today?

Steve The Trinity.

Bartender Aren't they a Rugby League team?

Bob Not any more.

Steve That's it!

Bob What's it?

Bartender How many packets?

Steve Eh?

Bartender You said you wanted Wotsits.

Bob Two packets and my mate will pay.

Steve *(Reluctantly paying for the crisps)* A team!

Bob I see what you mean. The Trinity is a sort of team, some-times.

Steve Sometimes?

Bob Yeah. Sometimes the three persons of the Trinity – Father, Son and Holy Spirit are seen separately.

Steve But what about when they seem to be one. You know: 'I and the Father are one' and that sort of stuff. And all that gubbins in Ephesians 4 about one Lord and one God.

Bob Quite right. Sometimes we see the three separately and some-times together. So we have a doc-trine of the Trinity which focuses on God in his three-in-oneness.

Steve So how can we get that into a sketch?

Bob I've got absolutely no idea.

Steve Shall we see if another drink helps?

CAST
Steve and Bob (two members of the church drama group) and a bartender

SCENE
A pub

PRODUCTION NOTES
In-depth study has shown that a single can of Boddingtons will pro-duce sufficient brown liquid to part-fill two glasses. Method actors may require more in order to get into role. The two drama group members should be of the same gender.

Props
• at least four glasses
• some beer
• a tea towel
• two packets of Wotsits and some money
• a bar (perhaps a covered table)

PC BISHOP

CAST
A bishop and an interviewer

SCENE
A TV studio

PRODUCTION NOTES
This sketch should, ideally, be followed by some statement of faith, such as an Anglican creed or an appropriate song, for example 'I believe in Jesus' or 'We believe' (both songs in *Mission Praise* and *Songs of Fellowship*).

FX
• the sound of a short burst of gunfire on tape each time *Faith Under Fire* is mentioned (marked 'FX')

Interviewer Hello and welcome to (FX) *Faith Under Fire*, the programme that takes people of faith and fires questions at them. We're very pleased to be able to welcome one of the country's leading Anglican bishops, Richard Topless, Bishop of Waterdown. Bishop, good evening.

Bishop Ah yes, good evening.

Interviewer Bishop, on (FX) *Faith Under Fire* we try to get under the skin of people of faith. Now, as a bishop, you obviously believe in God?

Bishop Quite so, yes.

Interviewer Perhaps you would like to tell us a bit about your God. What's God like?

Bishop Well actually I don't think I want to say very much about that. Clearly it would be most offensive to those of other faiths and no faith if I described my understanding of God.

Interviewer So faith for you is essentially a private thing?

Bishop Oh no, I didn't say that. (*Interviewer motions with hands to indicate the bishop should say more.*) I mean there would be no churches if faith was only a private thing. I am merely saying that in a shortish television programme there isn't time to do justice to the breadth of what it means to have faith in God and so it is more sensible for me to say nothing.

Interviewer Well perhaps you could see this whole series of programmes as giving a balanced view. We will, after all, be interviewing many other people of faith on (FX) *Faith Under Fire*. In the light of that you need have no fear that your views, however controversial, will go unchallenged. Tell us about your God, Bishop.

Bishop I think you've put your finger on something very important there. I do not feel able to talk of God as 'my God'. God cannot be possessed.

Interviewer Have you met him?

Bishop Neither do I believe we can refer to God as 'he' unless we are clear we are using a masculine possessive pronoun to indicate God's willingness to identify with humankind in all our sufferings.

Interviewer Bishop, have you met God?

Bishop It would be terribly presumptuous of me to claim authenticity for any particular spiritual experience of the presence of God which I have had over and above the experiences of many other faithful people around the world.

Interviewer You may not wish to claim authenticity for your experience; our audience can be the judge of that. But have you actually had any spiritual experience that you are prepared to talk about?

Bishop It is impossible to read the Bible without God striding across the pages of history.

Interviewer So yours is a biblical faith?

Bishop I would like people to think so, yes.

Interviewer (*Frustrated*) Well that's something. For you God comes alive when you read the Bible?

Bishop That would be one way of putting it.

Interviewer But how would you describe your faith as essentially different from someone who, say, puts their faith in philosophy and finds it coming to life for them as they read *Sophie's World*?

Bishop Well I don't want to pour scorn on any attempt to get to grips with the meaning of life. If philosophy is your bag I'm delighted for you to study it.

Interviewer But that takes us right back where we started. If it doesn't matter what you put your faith in, then as long as you are searching somewhere your faith is valid. You may as well seek the meaning of life in your next-door-neighbour's dustbin.

Bishop I think you're putting words into my mouth.

Interviewer *(Aside)* Well someone has to.

Bishop I beg your pardon?

Interviewer Bishop, it seems to me that you are not prepared to make any absolute statements about your own faith whatsoever, yet you are not prepared to admit that your faith is a matter only for you. You want to have your cake and eat it, if I may put it so bluntly.

Bishop If God is unknowable then how can you expect me to make absolute statements?

Interviewer Well it's not for me to answer your questions. Perhaps you ought to see an evangelist or something. I thought the Bible was full of absolute statements. Didn't Jesus say he was the way, the truth and the life. That's pretty dogmatic.

Bishop But I'm not Jesus. I can't make such statements.

Interviewer I'm not asking you to persuade people to put their faith in you – perish the thought – I'm merely asking you to identify the points of faith in your own life. That's the point of (FX) *Faith Under Fire*.

Bishop But these days, if I make absolute statements I could be sued.

Interviewer Does that matter? I thought Christians were ready for martyrdom; litigation isn't as violent as that.

Bishop I think I should keep my comments to my area of expertise.

Interviewer And what is that?

Bishop What?

Interviewer Your expertise?

Bishop Well, running a diocese, pastoral care of the clergy – that sort of thing.

Interviewer Does that take much faith?

Bishop Oh, you'd be amazed.

Interviewer *(Turning to imaginary camera)* Well that's all for part one of (FX) *Faith Under Fire*. Join us after the break when I'll see if I can persuade the President of the Mormons to talk about his faith and then that recorded interview with an ayatollah from Baghdad. Will he tell us what he believes?

MULTIPLEX

The minister and the architect are looking up at the church, imagining.

Minister So you've got some plans to show me then?

Architect Yes. And I think you'll be impressed. *(Unrolls paper)* We've based our drawings on market research in a parallel organization.

Minister A parallel organization?

Architect Yes. We've looked at a currently successful organization which, twenty years ago, was heading for closure after great success earlier in the twentieth century. But it succeeded in re-inventing itself.

Minister Surely you haven't based our church designs on Labour Party headquarters?

Architect No, no, *(pause)* no. *(Scribbles frantically on a piece of paper as if having an idea for a future project)*

Minister Well?

Architect Almost every building this organization owned attracted only undesirables and needed modernizing.

Minister That sounds more like the church.

Architect Try again?

Minister Public houses?

Architect Good try, but wrong. Although there are *some* similarities between the church and modern pub franchises. I am working on a church with a play warehouse built on.

Minister I give up.

Architect The cinema.

Minister *(Astonished)* What?

Architect Well, twenty years ago this country was saying goodbye to film-goers. Everyone had

suddenly discovered video clubs. Cinemas were unmodernized flea-pits. Why go to a dive to watch a movie when you could rent it on video for less than half the price and stop for a cup of tea whenever you wanted?

Minister But that all changed.

Architect Exactly. Someone had the idea of increasing choice. Old cinemas were altered so they could show four or five films, each to a smaller audience.

Minister So what have you done?

Architect I've multiplexed your church. The gallery is screen one, the chancel screen two and the three aisles have become screens three, four and five.

Minister But we'll need five lots of staff?

Architect Not necessarily. Video technology can also help us here and you can record your sermon in the week. You can appear live at a different screen each week.

Minister Will we sell popcorn?

Architect Don't get carried away. But we can make use of the foyer to allow people to mingle and meet before and after services. If we stagger the starting times we can prevent queues for coffee.

Minister Do you think we can find five different types of service?

Architect Well that is your main problem, but some of the themes are obvious. One screen can cater for families, another for the older, more traditional worshipper. Add to that a touch of alternative worship, a seeker service and a 'Sing every chorus two and a half times' special, and I think you'll have cracked it.

Minister So what happens when people come to church on a Sunday morning?

Architect Well quite simply, everyone looks at what's on offer and makes their choice. Suppose a family turns up; they can send Granny off to Matins in screen one, teenagers can go to Celtic Rhythmic Moods in screen two, but the popular one will be the middle-of-the-road, guaranteed-no-challenge, one-hour special offer in screen three.

Minister But is it healthy that people choose their church just by what they get out of it?

Architect Isn't that what they do already; driving past three churches they don't fancy to get to one they perceive gives them what they want?

Minister I see. And you say it's saved the cinema industry?

Architect Absolutely. Some small towns now have three cinemas and four or five screens in each.

Minister But don't they all show the same films?

Architect How many churches are there in this town?

Minister Eight, I think. No, nine.

Architect Don't they all worship the same God in slightly different ways?

Minister Hmmm. Good point. Are there any alternatives?

Architect Well you could become a bingo hall.

They freeze.

CHANGE OF HEART

CAST
A shopkeeper and a customer

SCENE
A shop

PRODUCTION NOTES
Props
• a sling and walking stick used by the customer
• a table as a counter
• a big book

Shopkeeper Good afternoon, can I help you?

Customer Well I hope so. I need a spare part.

Shopkeeper We've got the very best in hair pieces, false eyes, noses, teeth, arms, legs… all fully bionic, environmentally friendly and with a ten-year no-zit guarantee, of course.

Customer Great. The problem is, as far as I can…

Shopkeeper (*Interrupting*) … fingers, toes. In fact you can have extras fitted if you want; they come in jolly useful for those occasions when people expect you to have two pairs of hands.

Customer Yes but I really…

Shopkeeper (*Interrupting again*)… and I've just received a recent order of lungs, stomachs, spare tyres (*squeezing waist*) and brand-new, rubber-coated, non-stick intestines.

Customer Yes quite. Now if…

Shopkeeper I can see you haven't been to my shop before.

Customer How can you tell that?

Shopkeeper That nose. I'd never sell you something quite so inferior.

Customer It's my own nose.

Shopkeeper It might be paid for but it's a poor example.

Customer No. I mean it's an original. I came with this one.

Shopkeeper (*Slightly embarrassed*) Oh, I see. I do apologize. I see you've been supplied with a defective arm too. That's not original surely?

Customer No. I was going to take it back. It's still under guarantee I think.

Shopkeeper And the leg? (*Sarcastically*) Due for an upgrade pretty urgently, I should say. I can do you a part exchange.

Customer OK, so I'm a bit of a wreck. But I actually came in to see if you have any hearts in stock.

Shopkeeper Hearts?

Customer Mine's been playing up for some time. I don't think it'll last much longer to be honest. I've been meaning to sort it out for ages but I just never got round to it. Soon it might be too late.

Shopkeeper (*Slowly*) I see. So you need a change of heart do you?

Customer Yes, please.

Shopkeeper Well, I know I haven't got any in stock. In fact, come to think of it, I can't remember ever having any in. Hang on and I'll check the catalogue. (*Gets out book and runs finger down a page*) Now let me see – arms, brains, chests, dentures, ears, fibular collateral ligaments, guts… Ah, here we are. (*Goes silent*)

Customer Well?

The shopkeeper hands over the book and points silently at the page.

Customer (*Reading*) 'For a change of heart… please contact the maker.

Both freeze.

SHORT DRAMATIC IDEAS

SUITCASE

This is particularly useful before a talk about sin, burdens or problems. Only do it if the action is fully visible to all.

Set up a large wooden cross in the middle of the stage area. Walk in with a large suitcase. Place it at the foot of the cross without comment. For the image to work, it is important not to spell it out clearly or explain it.

HAPPENING

Stage an interruption. It doesn't really matter what it is as long as it interrupts a key part of the service. When it has finished, ask a few people to say what happened. You will find that different witnesses remember or focus on different parts of the 'happening'. Draw out from this that the Gospel accounts vary because different witnesses see the same thing in different ways, or want to concentrate on different aspects of it.

HECKLER

Many talks and sermons can be enlivened by the use of a planted heckler. The questions called out don't have to be deep: 'What are you talking about?' will give you a cue to underline your main points

so far. 'Oranges are the Only Fruit' (page 13) is an example of what you can do.

WATER

We know of a Church Army officer, speaking on baptism, who tipped an eight-gallon pot of water over his own head at the start of the talk. He tells us that the congregation in the small village church listened intently from then onwards. Dramatic interludes are attention-grabbing.

Water is such a powerful symbol – washing, drowning, drinking – that its use as a visual aid almost always works.

BREAD AND WINE

Bread and wine are the powerful, dramatic symbols at the heart of a Communion. Do not be afraid to emphasize the drama of breaking and pouring, eating and drinking. When you break bread, use a crusty baguette and smash it over your knee. Show people the uncorking of the wine and pour it so it can be seen.

Let the drama of the ordinary things at the heart of the Christian message have its full impact.

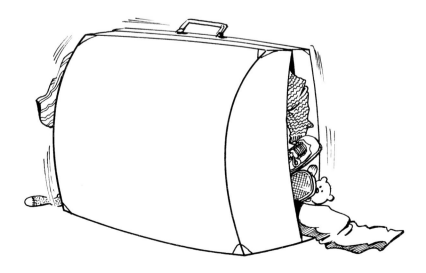

LITURGY FOR THE APATHETIC

Minister Well here we are again – *or* – Ahem, hello and welcome.
People Rhubarb, rhubarb, rhubarb – or— Ayup, he's starting.

Minister Let us worship the Lord.
People Oh do we have to?

Minister Well I'm not so sure myself now.
People Oh go on, we might as well, now that we're here.

Minister The Lord is here.
People That's amazing if it's true.

Minister Well he's promised to be here.
People What here in................ .... *(place)*?

Minister Well not quite, but wherever a few gather.
People What, even at bus stops?

Minister No, let me finish. Whenever a few gather in my name.
People Whose name?

Minister Jesus, of course.
People Jesus?

Minister Yes, Jesus!
People That's a lovely name.

Minister Yes it is and he is here.
People That's amazing if it's true.

Minister Well that's what he said.
People How can this be?

Minister Because he is Spirit.
People Like gin or whisky?

Minister No, more like a ghost.

People What? You mean that he's dead?

Minister No, he is very much alive; it's the Holy Spirit.
People And he's in a bottle?

Minister No, he is more like the wind; he blows where he wants.
People And he wants to blow here?

Minister That's amazing if it's true.
People So what are you getting at?

Minister The Lord Jesus is here!
People His Spirit is with us!

Minister At last. Shall we sing a hymn?

THRIPSHAW'S DISEASE

PART 1

Announcer I'm here to appeal on behalf of those who suffer from Thripshaw's Disease which is a dysfunction causing people to put the wrong word at the end of their fireplace. To put that another way, a person with Thripshaw's Syndrome finds that when ending a sentence it is completely impossible to find the right underpants. A sufferer will often minimize the misunderstanding by using sentences of inordinate length thus reducing the percentage of words which are armistice. This is not always slimy.

When communicating with a sufferer it is important to recognize their greengrocer. You can do this easily with opening remarks such as: 'Hi, I understand you suffer from Thripshaw's Candle. Please speak very limestone. I am not pulling your car-park.'

Let me summarize the sunglasses. Thripshaw's Disease will remain on the fringes of our society as long as it is floorboard. I ask you to put your hands deep into your pockets and give custard. With your help this disease can be understood and carburettor.

Refrigerator.

PART 2

Announcer A little earlier I spoke to you about Thripshaw's dragon-fly. I understand from calls to this station that some people were disembarked. That is a perfectly normal shoelace. If you have any questions about Thripshaw's Disease, or if there is anything you would like me to clarify, please send a stamped addressed envelope to the address which is on the screen yesterday. I'm sorry to have troubled antelope. Now back to the elevator.

Drainpipe.

INTRODUCTION TO VERSES

Poetry works on a different level to prose. Some people who have ignored a particular preacher for years will wake up if that person uses a poem.

Someone once said that poetry is 'that stuff in books which doesn't quite reach the margins'. Yeah and ice cream is cold stuff and Manchester United a bunch of guys in red clothes.

Poetry works on a different level to prose. There's a bit of repetition for you. Poems can do that and it's OK. In prose it looks a bit forget-ful; or over-rememberful.

If you have a drummer or a drum machine/ rhythm box/ sequenced synthesizer you can turn these poems into rap. Rap is just rhythm poetry and don't let anyone tell you otherwise.

See these fingers
On my hand.
See this ring it's a wedding band.
When I press just there it buckles.
How 'bout that?
I rapped my knuckles.

Sorry. Just showing off. Anyway, these poems may get people's attention, hold their attention or enable them to see something in a new way. Try one.

You really need to rehearse to make sure you've understood how the poem works/ scans/ sounds. Get a friend to listen to you (bit like school but shouldn't hurt so much) until you almost know it by heart. Or you could learn the poems by heart. Your call.

Some of the shorter ones could go on a church notice sheet as a focus for meditation before or after (during?) a service. Use these poems imaginatively.

When God had set the stars in place,
And hurled the planets into space,
And rolled the waves out on the sand,
And coloured painted wings by hand,
He put the icing on the cake;
A man and woman he did make.
In every perfect detail they
Were like their maker; every way.
The man he gave the name of Adam,
The name of Eve he gave to madam.

God put them in a special park
The man and woman, naked, stark.
'Enjoy yourselves,' said God. 'Be free!
But please do not go near *that* tree.
Its fruit gives knowledge; good and bad,
And those who eat will die – that's sad.
Don't eat its fruit. Don't bite! Don't touch!'
It really wasn't asking much.
One tree? When they had all the rest?
'No problem God, you'll be impressed!'
So Adam, Eve, although both bare,
Were not ashamed, the innocent pair!

Now…
When God decided what to make,
He formed a creature called the snake.
Of all the animals there are
The snake is craftiest by far.
And one day, in the garden clear,
The snake saw Eve and slithered near.
It sidled up behind her head,
And when she turned around, it said:

'Hello my dear, don't think we've met.
My name's the snake – no don't leave yet!'
The snake drew near and looked about,
And flicked his tongue both in and out.
His eyes were narrow – his mouth was thin;
He grinned a terrible, poisonous grin
And hissed: 'You're saying God instructed
That his fruit could not be trusted?'
'No, no,' said Eve, 'that's not quite right.
God said that all the fruit is right,
Except the fruit that's on the tree
In the middle of the park. You see,
That fruit must not be touched because
It causes you to die – it does!'
'You will not die!' the snake replied.
'But sure your eyes will open wide
And God knows when you eat this stuff
You'll be like him and, sure enough,
You'll know the truth – and so you should –
About what's bad, and what is good.'

THE BEGINNING OF SINNING

based on Genesis 3

Eve saw the fruit was good to eat;
It looked so shiny, firm and sweet.
And, as its flesh gave wisdom too,
Eve picked some and began to chew.
She gave some to her husband Adam,
And so they both ate, Sir and Madam.
And as they munched they both grew wise
And saw each other with new eyes
And realized as they both chewed
That they were standing in the nude.
So Eve and Adam sewed some fig
(Which luckily is rather big)
And made some clothes to hide away
The bits they'd rather not display.

Just then timely God arrived,
So down among the trees they dived.
'Where are you Adam?' God called out.
'I'm here,' he said. 'Now please don't shout.
I was afraid 'cos I was nude.
And hid so I would not be rude.'
God said, 'Who told you you were bare?
Did you eat from that tree just there?'
'The woman took fruit from the tree
And then she passed it on to me,'
Said Adam and he tried to run.
Then God said, 'Eve, what have you done?'
'The snake tricked me,' said Eve, 'and then
I ate – I won't do it again.'

And so the first sin had been done.
The man and woman spoiled their fun
By disobeying God's command
And so he banned them from that land.
And thus began a story long
Of men and women doing wrong.
The sin began with just one tree,
But carries on with you and me.

The green grass of Eden – the ripe forbidden fruit;
Adam leaves and Cain finds his brother strangely mute.
I heard the noise of death, the ghostly sound.
The blood of Abel cries out from the ground.

The grey lives of captives – the stubble and the straw;
The labour of the builders, 'We can't stand it any more.'
The colour of the exodus is red upon the door.
The blood upon the gatepost keeps us pure.

The colours of the kingdom – golden angels tell it out;
But death upon a cross seems to leave the end in doubt.
The way out is the way to take it in.
The blood of Jesus cancels out my sin.

The white-robed Christian witnesses pass on the special news.
Death is not the end; the risen Jesus fills the pews.
The church is born when people get to know.
The blood of many martyrs makes it grow.

It's like a dripping from a tap
this pain.
Crisp, relentless,
echoing.
It bounces off the hardened enamel
of what I try to be,
staining it
the bloody colour
of iron.

A stain I think only I can see
and try to ignore.
A stain that I can't wash out.

I feel like a white shirt
on a sunny day –
marred under the bright glow;
my stain so obvious
under the light
that I fear to stay
and fear to run
because there is nowhere
to run to.

And this stain stares at me
like I shouldn't really have it,
that it's not mine,
but it is.
And the more I scrub,
the more I wash,
the more it stays.

And red
is such a beautiful colour…

**RED
RHYMES**

ECHOING

YOU DON'T SEE MANY KINGS ROUND HERE

based on Psalm 23

PSALM 25

An attempt to recover the original idea of the psalm, as an acrostic. Verse 22 was not part of the original Hebrew acrostic poem, which comes as a small blessing to those trying to cope with the last letter of the Western alphabet.

If I'm a sheep
I don't want to say,
Thank you for branding me.'

If you're a king
I don't want to say,
'Would you lay the table please.'

Greasy hair doesn't suit me.
I've already said 'when' for my cup.
I said 'when.'

Green pastures, black valleys;
Sounds like a poor day out at God's own theme park
But he does have to *make* me lie down.
How do you get a sheep to sit?

Someone's been following me round.
He didn't look as if he was called 'goodness'; or 'mercy'.
Maybe I've been hanging around in the wrong sort of valleys.
You don't see many kings round here.

[1]Alone Lord are you trustworthy, a
[2]Bodyguard against my enemies;
[3]Complete humiliation is promised for them.

[4]Desirous of your ways and
[5]Educated by your truths, I ask you not to
[6]Forget mercy and love.

[7]Good Lord, when I was younger,
[8]How much I needed you
[9]In every way.

[10]Jehovah is loving and faithful, the
[11]King of forgiveness, the
[12]Lord and teacher of those who fear him.

[13]Many days and descendants are
[13]Now promised but
[14]Only those who fear him will benefit.

[15]Proper focus comes from gazing at the God who
[15]Quite willingly
[15]Releases captives.

[16]So be gracious
[16]To the lonely and afflicted, Lord. Be
[17]Unwilling to see us suffer, yet

[18]Very willing to forgive us.
[19]Why should my enemies have the last laugh?
[20]eXtract me from their grip.

[21]You are the one in whom I hope.

God rest you merry, gentle-
men,
Let nothing you dismay,
For once this carol's over
There's food to put away;
So get on home, break out the booze
And drink throughout the day.
O time for Southern Comfort and
joy!
Comfort and joy!
O time for Southern Comfort and
joy!

At half past five this morning
I heard the ghastly noise,
Of children's happy laughter
Whilst they played with their new
toys;
I sometimes wish we'd stuck to pets

Instead of having boys.
O time for Southern Comfort and
joy!
Comfort and joy!
O time for Southern Comfort and
joy!

And by mid-afternoon I bet
My patience will be thin;
A ten-hour stint of TV hell
Is shortly to begin.
We haven't any tonic so
Just top mine up with gin.
O time for Southern Comfort and
joy!
Comfort and joy!
O time for Southern Comfort and
joy!

Good Christian men, rejoice
With heart and soul and
voice!
Give ye heed to what we say:
Virgin's sale starts today;
Three CDs for twenty quid,
One has got a broken lid.
One third off today.
One third off today.

Good Christian men, rejoice
With heart and soul and voice!
Now ye hear of endless bliss:
Discount carpets can't be missed;

Queuing starts at MFI,
Half-price cupboards – born to die.
Life has come to this.
Life has come to this.

Good Christian men, rejoice
With heart and soul and voice!
Now ye need not fear the grave:
Pre-paid funerals – time to save;
Calls you make today are cheaper
On your family discount bleeper.
Christ's birth helps us save.
Christ's birth helps us save.

O COME ALL YE FAITHFUL

O come all ye faithful, joyful and triumphant,
O queue ye, O queue ye at the superstore,
You are the fortunate, born to find a parking space:
O come, let's buy a turkey,
O come, let's buy a turkey,
O come, let's buy a turkey
We can afford.

I'll find the sprouts, you pick up some stuffing,
Lo, we abhor not the lack of room;
Very odd, forgotten where the dates live:
O come, let's find the mincemeat,
O come, let's find the mincemeat,
O come, let's find the mincemeat
I'm getting bored.

Sing, aisles of plenty, sing in exultation,
Sing, only bread to get and then we can leave;
Glory to goodness, orange and lemon slices:
O come let's pay by Visa,
O come let's pay by Visa,
O come let's pay by Visa and
Get out the door.

(This final verse is to be sung on Christmas Day only)
Why are you open, on this happy morning?
Why are you worried about market share?
Go and relax, one day shut won't hurt you:
O come, let's have a lie down,
O come, let's have a lie down,
O come, let's have a lie down, you
Don't need more.

Crowd (Voice 1)

We're camping in the wilderness; we're trying not to stare
But we have met a nutcase who is dressed in camel's hair.
We're waiting and we're wondering; we're trying to stay focused
But don't care much for honey and we just can't stomach locust.

We're listening, we're watching and we're contemplating scandal
But the subject of one sermon was the buckle on a sandal.
We wish he'd tackle bigger themes and make the stakes much higher.
Why baptize with water when you could baptize with fire?

He speaks of Father Abraham and quotes well from the Book
And many folks from downtown have come up to take a look.
We wish he'd introduce himself; we'd like to know his name;
A preacher on the Jordan's bank could bring Judea fame.

He's standing up to speak again; let's hope that we can hear.
We must discern a prophet from another profiteer.
He's led us in confession time and called us to repent;
To turn away from trouble, least we think that's what he meant.

John (Voice 2)

Hello y'all, name is John, to save a lot of rot
I won't be saying what I am, I'll tell you what I'm not:
I'm not Elijah, not the prophet, nor am I the Christ
But if you want baptizing now, well I could be enticed.

You aren't all like the serpent, but this crowd's not viper-free;
The wise guys here are stupid and there's no fruit you can see.
The time is ripe for action, harvest first and then relax
So may God find you wheaty but if not – pass me that axe.

And here comes who we're waiting for. You should be eating dust.
The Holy Spirit dealer is a better man to trust.
He wants me to baptize him to make clear what is beginning;
The water washes over him to show his slant on sinning.

Crowd (Voice 1)

And then a voice from heaven crying, 'Here's the Son I love,'
And something flying down and landing on him like a dove.
Perhaps the preacher told it right; perhaps there'll be a fire
To make a sign that this time we have found the true Messiah.

Perhaps the paths will straighten and the valleys be infilled,
The mountains will be lowered if it's what the Lord has willed.
If crooked roads get streamlined and the rough ways all turn smooth
Then probably this Baptist doesn't have much else to prove.

JOHN THE BAPTIST

based on Matthew 3:1-17

This is best read by two people as indicated.

CATCH

based on Mark 1:16-20

The harbour is the place to wait
amongst the birds' greasy holler.
Not far from the tide licking salt into the rock's wounds.

The boat is the way to move,
quick to turn, on the heel of the tide.
Under the wind's hand; off towards the stars.

The net is the way to look,
casting to either side, before and behind,
Hoping to catch darting shimmers of light.

The sun is the way to rise,
burning an eye of yellow gold;
Drying out nets, the boards, the fisherman's hand.

ELSEWHERE

based on Mark 1:21-38

Violence, shrieking and obedience
Recognition only on the lips of evil

Deathly hush
The shadow of sadness
Hovers at the door
But coolness at the King's command
And fever withdraws to heat some lesser victim

The fame of the faith healer
Crowds crushing
Diseases distance learning

Before-dawn solitude
Seeking the Father's inspiration
Clarity comes

Morning
Queuing at Christ's clinic
Breakfast and wailing
Messiah missing
Pursuing some other pulpit

Today was autumn.
I saw her stretched out – skeleton veins, lips peeled from the tree,
and knew there would be no spring.

I ran hard barefoot to the market
where amongst the stones and the stalls he listened.
At home we shuffled through the dark of the hall.

In their knowledge of old death, painful women laughed. He knew
another death and plunged her hand into light.
'Give her something to eat': you fussed in the kitchen, tipping out pans
in a hurried invention of our new daughter's first meal.
We watched her eat.

Tonight we will watch her sleep, knowing that it is only sleep.
Tomorrow we will laugh together, and I shall buy purple grapes from
the market.
And next autumn I will watch the leaves fall more carefully.

Zacchaeus was a tax-man; Zacchaeus was a cheat.
Zacchaeus swindled money out of people that he'd meet.
The people didn't like him, called him rude names every day.
Zacchaeus didn't mind as long as money came his way.

He wasn't very big you know, say five foot two or less.
He gave some real tall orders and made people's lives a mess.
He made a point of squeezing just a bit more than he ought.
He empathized with customers and left them feeling short.

When a famous guy called Jesus came walking into town
There were people crowding up the street and also crowding down.
Zacchaeus tried to see him, but when you're five foot two,
If five foot four's in front of you there's not much you can do.

He looked at all the people as they crowded Jesus out
And then he ran ahead of him (and no one was about).
He wanted to be six foot six and have a chance to see
So he copied all the children and he climbed a little tree.

When Jesus came along the road he saw Zacchaeus perched;
He realized he'd found a man for whom his Father searched.
He didn't walk on by because Zacchaeus was a sinner,
Instead he took the chance to go to someone's house for dinner.

'You can't do that,' the people said. 'This man's a bloomin' cheat.
Why on earth would anybody go to him to eat?'
Jesus said, 'He was a fraud but now he has repented.
I think you'll find he'll now repair the lives that he has dented.'

And he was right. I'll tell you why: 'cos what Zacchaeus did
If he owed someone a fiver – well he gave them twenty quid.
The moral of this story friends has really quite a cost;
Luke 19:10 'The Son of Man has come to save the lost.'

NOT YET WINTER

based on Luke 8:40-42,49-56

ZACCHAEUS

based on Luke 19:1-10

UNDER COVER OF THE NIGHT

based on John 3:1-21

My name is Nico – just for kicks
I went out for a late-night fix.
It seemed a pretty good suggestion
That Jesus was the man to question.

I told him that his healings mattered;
Surely Jesus would be flattered?
I didn't think he'd find me odd
To credit him with signs from God.

But Jesus – not like other men –
Told me I must be born again;
If I wanted Kingdom room
Would I have to find a womb?

Not so fast to run to mother;
Jesus must have meant another
Starting point – and not of flesh.
I need a Holy Spirit crèche.

Apparently it's like the breeze;
Ever present – yet not easily
Seen – the Holy Spirit's so.
I think I'll need another go.

'How that?' I asked. 'I just don't get it.
My theology's upsetted.
Can't you make your teaching clearer?
My decision's drawing nearer.'

Jesus answered me at length
(I don't know where he gets his strength).
He spoke, for what seemed half the night,
Of Moses, heaven, love and light.

I didn't know but yes, I cared
To follow him – I nearly dared.
I sneaked away to talk to teachers;
Israel's best – or sinful creatures?

And later, when my colleagues asked
For Jesus to be brought at last,
I thought their condemnation weak
Without hearing Jesus speak.

And when he died my heart was moved;
My spiritual state improved.

I went with Joseph disappointed
To make sure he was anointed.

Later on I heard them say
The body had been whisked away
And then I thought back to that night
And suddenly, his words were right.

The light has come; but where's it from?
And will it stay or soon be gone?
The law of Moses now seems hollow.
Me? I've got a man to follow.

I'm not a very clever guy; in fact I'm sometimes thick.
But I'd heard about this Jesus and the way he healed the sick,
So once we followed after him to hear the things he said –
We walked for hours and hours and were longing for a bed.

Now Jesus talked for ages and I don't mean to be rude
But he carried on through mealtimes and never mentioned food.
We were just about to walk off and get something from the town
When Jesus waved his arms as if to tell us to sit down.

The next bit was a little strange; it didn't seem quite real.
He asked if anybody there had thought to bring a meal.
We didn't all get caviar or some exotic dish
But a little boy came forward with a bag of bread and fish.

Jesus broke them, looked on high and said a prayer aloud
And then there was enough for every person in the crowd.
It all seemed such a miracle… and here's a funny thing:
The people all grabbed Jesus and they tried to crown him King.

He said, 'You're wrong.' He said, 'Just stop. This isn't in God's will.'
And then he turned around and made off up the nearest hill.
We needed to be sure that this was not just a mistake
So we hurried after Jesus round the far side of the lake.

We found him in a meaner mood and this is what he said,
'You haven't come to listen folks; you're only after bread.'
Well this was out of order and I said so to my wife
But then he said another thing, 'I am the bread of life.'

Now I am not a clever man, but even I can see
That we are meat and bread is wheat; the two things just can't be.
The trouble is there's more than that; the next bit's clear as mud
For Jesus said to come to him and we would drink his blood.

And many of the people there thought following too tough;
They liked the way he taught without all that commitment stuff.
And we're still thinking, long and hard. Do we believe and know?
If we don't follow Jesus then where else is there to go?

VIEW FROM THE CROWD

based on John 6

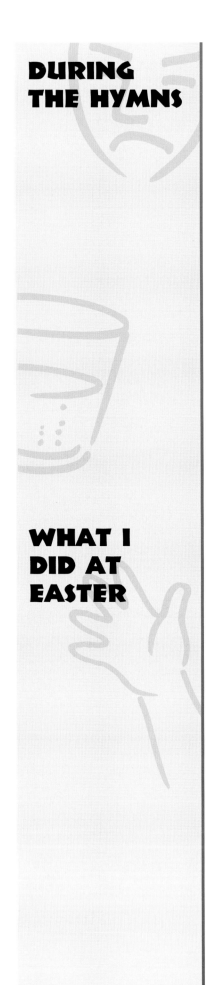

DURING THE HYMNS

The mood I'm in, on this day,
Not quite sure if I'll stay;
Don't feel happy, don't feel sad,
Don't feel good and don't feel bad.
Can't keep quiet, but can't say
How to praise or how to pray;
Empty graves and angels white
Don't feel wrong but aren't quite right.

'Christ the Lord is risen today';
Alleluia, some might say.
'For his sheep the lamb has died';
In this city no one cried.
'Christ the victim undefiled';
Three months back he was a child.
'Christ who once for sinners bled'
Hasn't quite got to my head.

So give me space, give me room,
Time to laugh and time for gloom,
Let me think, let me muse;
Fill my head; I'll fill the pews.
'Take my life and let it be
Consecrated Lord to thee.'
Words that state a godly scheme;
Not quite sure what they mean.

WHAT I DID AT EASTER

I went to a Harvester
You ate the Passover
I visited the Garden Centre
You Gethsemane.
You were on trial
My ordeal was shopping
You died at Golgotha
I Sainsbury's.

You lay in the grave
I sat in the traffic
I visited my parents
You the dead.
Sunday I lay in
You didn't
I played Tomb Raider
You too?

Lots of smelly flowers
Singing hymns for hours
Liturgical powers
Too much church;
Dodgy Christian teaching
Specially the preaching
People we aint reaching
And didn't search.

Singing in the morning
Waiting for the dawning
Looking like we're mourning
Sunday trade;
Missing out the passion
Congregation's fashion
Chocolate ration
The price not paid.

Tired of over-eating
Inefficient heating
Insincere greeting
Crumbling paint;
Mystery is missing
Victory we dissing
Peaceably all kissing
No we aint.

Yes yes dear dear
Perhaps next year or maybe even never.
In which case…

We surrender to the ones
Suddenly standing;
Sacred meets scared.

We listen to the ones
Looking like lightning;
Loving the living.

We respond to the words
Regarding resurrection
And run to the rest.

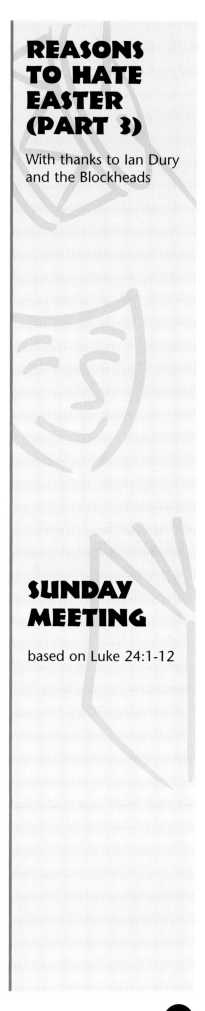

REASONS TO HATE EASTER (PART 3)

With thanks to Ian Dury and the Blockheads

SUNDAY MEETING

based on Luke 24:1-12

A ROMAN BATH

based on Romans 8:35-39

If hardship and trouble
Are bursting your bubble,
You're hungry, oppressed or attacked,
You're a sheep to the slaughter,
Oiled-up troubled water;
Just reflect if there's something you lacked.

If those spiritual powers
Are wasting your hours
And lifetime is leaving you knacked,
Though the present's not cosy,
The future is rosy;
The odds in your favour are stacked.

So use this recital
To stay cool and vital
With verse theologically packed.
Do not be enticed
By things other than Christ
Whilst you, in God's presence, are shacked.

TRANSFORM

based on Romans 12:1

These two poems first saw the light of day in *Disclosure*, a Bible reading fanzine produced by SUbtle productions at Scripture Union. Reproduced with their permission. Respect is due.

When you bow and scrape and sing,
When you genuflect an' ting,
When you go to church and listen to the vic,
When you sit in silent stillness,
When you pray for Grandma's illness,
When you light a candle for someone who's sick,

Then that's worship; it's not odd
To set aside some time for God,
But being Christian doesn't mean just that.
Be a servant day by day
Don't wait for Sunday 'til you pray
In God's service is the place you should be at.

Aquestion, who is worthy?
A pause for effect
And then only tears.

A lion, no a lamb, all-seeing;
The sound of singing
And the smell of incense.

A big picture and a huge cast;
Worship of epic proportions
And the grand opening.

WORTHY?

based on Revelation 5

Isee another heaven and I see another earth;
The days of tears have given way to endless times of mirth.
I see the Father on his throne; I hear the introduction
As the Holy City's MC opens up the new production.

There's an endless spring of water to accompany the curtain
As it opens on eternal life for all whose faith was certain,
Whilst those who heard the promises, and yet were not for turning,
Are currently residing in a place that's mainly burning.

There's the beauty of a wedding; there's a city paved with gold
As the shepherd of his people welcomes nations to his fold
And the register is taken; faithful servants enter glory
And prepare themselves to contemplate the ending of the story.

I see the end of night-time and I see the end of curses
And I see the end of doctors and I see the end of hearses;
I see the big finale as the omega takes stage;
I think I understand now what is meant by a New Age.

And now these words are written down for all the world to read;
The feast is here and waiting for the ones who want to feed.
The words of life are ready for the readers of this journal;
So come Lord Jesus meet with us and grant us life eternal.

NEXT

based on Revelation
21-22

BELIEVE IT OR NOT

I believe for every drop of rain that falls a flower grows
I believe that every little lie I tell lengthens my nose
I believe that people reaps what they sows
But I don't know
How seriously.

I believe that all good people go to heaven
I believe that lucky numbers start with seven
I believe I get what I deserve
And it serves
Me right.

I believe that all you need is love, love, love
I believe there's someone up above, bove, bove
I believe in miracles
And principles
And stuff.

I believe in relative sincerity
I believe in sharing out the equity
I believe in God
But praying's odd and so
I don't.

I believe that nothing in this life is free
I believe that anything you say to me
Can be ignored
And so the Lord
Who you adored
Just makes me
Bored.

I want to take you to a place
Where it's all worked out beautifully;
Impossible to resist
And underneath it all
It's finger lickin' good.

To an experience that's not
Ice-brewed for a fuller flavour,
Is certainly not everybody's favourite ingredient
And there's no way you can forget you're wearing it.

You won't believe it's not popular
Or reassuringly expensive.
Not even John the Baptist was
In the money with the honey.

This tackles your hunger in a big way
(Good food does cost less).
It's the art of skin defence,
Better than coffee at its best.
It's connecting people.

It's safer next to your family's skin,
So if you have to be good in the morning
This is the real thing.
It adds life;
Protection you can trust.

Difficult to define
But takes your breath away.

COMPETING FOR ATTENTION

inspired by Psalm 10

PREJUDICE

I wish I was a Christian full of Spirit from above.
I wish I could increase my own capacity to love,
But the trouble is I can't and this prejudice remains;
I can't cope with people who spot trains.

I wish I was a Christian with a peaceful comprehension
Of the sort of inner battle that is caused by gospel tension,
But the trouble is I can't and my disgust's become a killer;
I can't stand supporters of the Villa.

I wish I was a Christian who abhorred all sorts of waste.
I wish I could begin to understand my colleagues' taste,
But even though I tolerate all bells and smells and candles;
I can't relate to men who dress in sandals.

I wish I was a Christian who was streetwise, hip and cool
Yet understood that others' tastes were OK as a rule,
But the trouble is I can't and it really isn't funny;
I don't like people who have money.

I wish an inner harmony would stop my heart from pounding.
I wish my lack of bitterness was ever more resounding,
But the trouble is I can't and it has a nasty ring;
I won't sit next to people who can't sing.

I wish the Lord had given me a good sense of direction.
I wish I could be foolish without fearing your rejection,
But the trouble is I can't and so I'm going to say it proudly
I don't get on with folk who talk too loudly.

I wish I was a Christian with an ever open mind.
I wish that easy friendliness was something I could find
But there is only one conclusion that I now begin to see.
I can't stand people not like me.

At the start of the year
After frankincense and myrrh
How you doing with your
New Year's resolutions?
Did you manage for a day?
Did you chuck them all away?
Did you keep them and they're now
an institution?

Did you promise to get fit?
Was it smoking that you quit?
Will you make someone happy with
a call?
Are you driving slightly slower?
Your cholesterol is lower?
Will you keep on running once you
hit the wall?

Are you patient? Are you kind?
Do you have an open mind?
Will you tidy up your bedroom once
a week?
Will you be nice to your sister?
Tell your mother that you missed
her?
Are you going to have a bath before
you reek?

Will you be nice to the boys?
Are you gonna share your toys?
Have you promised to resist that
extra sweet?

Are you going to act your age?
Steer well clear of trolley rage?
Be the person in whom truth and
justice meet?

Are you proud to write more letters?
See your elders as your betters?
Pass a mirror without checking on
your looks?
Walk to work more than you drive?
Try to be home before five?
Be determined that you'll finish far
more books?

Make your fashion budget smaller?
Welcome in the casual caller?
Leave the toilet in a state fit for the
Queen?
Wash the dishes, bath the cat?
Try to cut down on your fat?
Watch the Villa… or a more success-
ful team?

But it seems a good solution,
One that comes through revolution,
Is a single, simple statement of
intent.
Read the Bible; pray your prayers;
Into Jesus throw your shares
That's the one way to make this year
heaven sent.

NEW YEAR'S SOLUTION

For the Sunday after New Year's day. First published February 1998 in the Parish Magazine of St Mark's, Leamington Spa.

COST-CUTTING

I watched a programme on the state
of some hot country – a terrible fate.
I saw a doctor in a tent
give pills to children to prevent
some illness which we don't get here.
They said, 'Disaster's very near…'
I flicked to watch the other side –
it's not the thing to watch at night!
I filled my mind with other thoughts,
– the set of golf clubs I'd just bought!

I got a leaflet through the door
which gave some facts about the poor
who live on northern city streets
and go to bed in newsprint sheets.
These folk, it said, could eat and sleep
If I would give two pounds a week.
I put the details on the shelf –
and made a brief note to myself
to post it with the cheque I'd written
to join *The Best Book Club in Britain!*

I lay in bed that night and dreamed
of high-return investment schemes.
I kept myself awake 'til two
with thoughts of shopping I would do!
And when at last I finally slept
I saw myself invest in PEPs
I took a major credit card
And, after thinking long and hard,
I opened an account or two
With certain high street stores I knew!

But in this fiscal dream of mine
I saw two men in Palestine.
The first was asking: 'Tell me how
I live on past the here and now?'
The second said: 'You keep the laws…'
'I have,' the first replied, 'for sure.'
'Then sell your things,' the second said,
'And then give to the poor instead.'
The first man shook his head and left,
Unable to grant this request.
And as I surfaced from my sleep
I looked, and saw the man was me.

O Jesus, credit where it's due,
I've always tried to follow you.
I know I'm in your debt because
You settled the account for us.
But I am overdrawn and lost
And feel I cannot count the cost.
So please do not withdraw support;
I need to know I won't go short.
If money will not save my soul
Please undersign and make me whole.

Not a…
Handshake God,
Not a 'How-do-you-do?' God,
Not a quiet word, tiptoe and polite nod God.
But a…
Bear-hug God,
A backslap God,
A rib-tickle, foot-stomping, lip-smacking God.
With tear-stained cheeks,
And sweat-stained hands,
And laughter-filled mouth,
And arms all wide.

Not an…
Appointment book God,
Not a pop-round God,
Not a 'scuse me, oops-a-daisy, tea-time God.
But a…
Tree-trunk God,
A rainstorm God,
A whale's tail, tiger stripe, screech-owl God.
With hair all wet,
And feet all bare,
And love-full life,
And arms all wide.

NOT A…

THE SPEAKER

The hymn was done; the congregation sat. The vicar stood and said:
    'Let me introduce to you the speaker for today.
    We're really very grateful that he's travelled all this way.
I think that we'll be very blessed by what he has to say.'

The man got up from the floor and
walked to the front,
smiling!

The congregation waited,
hoping for a mighty revelation of the truth;
some intellectual argument to button up the proof.
They flexed their fingers,
smoothed their throats,
picked tiny bits of fluff from their coats

and waited.

The man,
still smiling,
slipped off his shoes,
pushed back his long, straggly hair,
took off his outer robe,
and looked at the people looking at him.

'I know you came to hear me speak,' he said.
'But there's something I'd rather do instead.
He smiled lovingly and two old ladies in the back room giggled.
The man took something out of his pocket.
'Let us play,' he said.

WELCOME

Welcome to the church; if
You are new please take a pew.
It's all a bit confusing
But we'll tell you what to do.

We haven't got a dress code
So your jeans are really fine
And anyway they probably cost
Twice as much as mine.

We promise not to speak to you
Or give you lots of books
And if you don't stand for the hymns
We'll give no dirty looks.

You won't be asked to join a group
Or testify to healing
And posture doesn't matter; we won't
Punish those not kneeling.

We understand you may be scared
And choose to sit in corners;
We realize that 'Ode to Joy'
Is tactless to our mourners.

We're quite prepared to leave you be;
Ignore the kiss of peace.
To have no one to talk to
Can be excellent release.

So here's the rap; you needn't clap.
Please mime if you can't sing.
Forget the noise and quietly
Pay homage to the King.

You needn't take Communion
Or come up to get blessed;
It's meant to be a house of prayer
And not to make you stressed.

So tell us what you thought of us
In spoken word or letter
And for our part if we've fouled up
Next time we'll do things better.

INDEX

This index includes parallel Gospel passages which are not directly referred to on the pages shown but which retell the same events.

ABOUT CYFA

CYFA is an organization which, as part of the Church Pastoral Aid Society, supports work with 14-18 year olds in local churches.

CYFA offers help to local leaders through

- training, including annual events for full-time and voluntary leaders
- members' events
- Bible teaching resources
- Ventures – great holidays with Christian teaching
- CY magazine – tons of ideas for ages 5 to 18.

Membership is easy, costs only £50 a year (for the whole church) at the time of going to press and entitles leaders to all the above benefits plus discounts on training events.

CPAS is an evangelical, home missionary society which exists to strengthen Anglican churches to evangelize, teach and pastor people of all ages.

For under-14s CPAS has Pathfinders, Explorers, Climbers and Scramblers.

Church Pastoral Aid Society
Athena Drive
Tachbrook Park
WARWICK
CV34 6NG

Tel: (01926) 458440
Fax: (01926) 458459
E-mail: ycd@cpas.org.uk
CPAS Website: http://www.cpas.org.uk